D0605707

Paleo Bond
spray adhesive
••••••

SHELLAC

This BOOK belongs to

U.P.R.R.

Paleo TOOTHPASTE

Thanks to paleontologist Michael K. Brett-Surman, Ph.D, for touring me through Wyoming's Jurassic Morrison Formation,
as well as the back halls of Washington's Smithsonian National Museum of Natural History.
He answered zillions of my questions, silly and not. This book could not have been written without him.

Thanks also to Cliff and Row Manuel of Geoscience Adventures in Shell, Wyoming,
and to James Farlow, Ph.D, a paleontologist and authority on dinosaur tracks.

This one's for Carl and Sam.
My love always.

Copyright © 2011 by Jessie Hartland
All rights reserved / CIP data is available
Published in the United States 2011 by
🍎 Blue Apple Books
515 Valley Street, Maplewood, NJ 07040
www.blueapplebooks.com

First Edition
Printed in China 09/11
ISBN: 978-1-60905-090-0

1 3 5 7 9 10 8 6 4 2

Hartland, Jessie.
How the dinosaur got to
the museum /
2011.
33305223254289
ca   03/09/12

Jessie Hartland

HOW THE DINOSAUR GOT TO THE MUSEUM

Blue Apple Books

NATURAL SMITHSONIAN HISTORY

Millions and
millions of years ago,
dinosaurs had the run of
the Earth. They romped
in the sun, ate what they pleased,
and were bothered by no one
but one another.

More than 145 million years have
passed since *this* dinosaur died.
Over time, our planet
went through colossal changes—
icy glaciers formed, then melted;
forests rose up and died;
volcanoes erupted; storms raged—
causing this dinosaur's bones
to be hidden for
a long, long, long time.

The mighty  **DIPLODOCUS**,
an herbivore (plant-eater)
with pencil-like teeth,
grazes on the plain.

The rain comes—
dripping, drenching, pouring—
and turns into a torrential flood,
sweeping the big dinosaur off its feet,
down the river to its death.

As years turn into decades,
and decades into centuries,
sand and silt blow
over the dinosaur's bones,
burying them deeper
and deeper and deeper.

Sea levels rise and fall . . .

the earth cracks . . .

and powerful sand storms swirl
over the old river beds.

Millions more years go by.
Mountains uplift,
tilting the dinosaur beds.

Water and wind erode the rocks.

One hundred and forty-five million years
have passed after the river flooded and buried

the  ,

and the ancient river bed is finally exposed.

Here, rooting around the old river bed in 1923,

is the DINOSAUR HUNTER.

He has studied geology, pored over maps and books,

and knows roughly where to look for

dinosaur fossils. After searching and digging

for months and months, he finds

AN UNUSUALLY LARGE BONE

in what today we call Utah.

He suspects that what he has found MAY just be a leg bone from

a **DIPLODOCUS** longus.

Here is the **PALEONTOLOGIST,**

an expert in prehistoric fossils, who travels from the

Smithsonian Museum of Natural History in Washington, D.C.

to the plains of Utah to view the bone. He confirms that,

YES!, it is indeed a dinosaur bone, late Jurassic period,

most likely a tibia from the leg of the

DIPLODOCUS ,

which was . . .

SMITHSONIAN
Dept. of Geology
WASHINGTON, D.C.

discovered by the DINOSAUR HUNTER.

Here is the team of

EXCAVATORS,

from the Smithsonian, who remove

the tons of stone surrounding the specimen.

They work in the hot sun for over one year,

searching for, digging up, and numbering

more and more bones from the

 **DIPLODOCUS**, which was . . .

confirmed by the PALEONTOLOGIST
and spotted by the DINOSAUR HUNTER.

Here are the MOVERS,

who carefully pack the wagons,

haul to the train, and deliver

to the museum the multiple boxes of

the 145 million-year-old bones of the

DIPLODOCUS,

which was . . .

1502   UNION
PACIFIC

15

U.P.R

24

17   31   7

dug up by the EXCAVATORS,

identified by the PALEONTOLOGIST

and found by the observant DINOSAUR HUNTER.

Tibia   BOX 2

Here are the PREPARATORS in the old Department of Geology
at the Smithsonian's National Museum of Natural History in Washington, D.C.,
who unpack all 34 boxes, and dust off and
shellac each bone until they discover . . .

DIPLODOCUS

BZ4

12

A,B

1,2,3,7

CAUDAL VERTEBRAE
27

HUMERUS
4

OH, NO!
The head and neck
are missing!

As quick as can be,
the **CURATOR**

makes numerous phone calls,

sends multiple letters and

several dozen telegrams marked

"SUPER-URGENT!" to other museums.

He tracks down a replacement plaster cast

of the missing head and neck for the

DIPLODOCUS,

which was . . .

located at the Carnegie Museum in Pittsburgh, Pennsylvania

and shipped as quickly as possible to the Smithsonian Museum in Washington, D.C.

The crates arrive—at last!—and assembly is resumed on the

DIPLODOCUS , which was . . .

unpacked by the PREPARATORS,

packed in wagons by the MOVERS,

uncovered by the EXCAVATORS,

verified by the PALEONTOLOGIST

and located by the DINOSAUR HUNTER.

FIG NEWTONS

A-Z

Here again are the PREPARATORS, now aided by

the PALEONTOLOGISTS, who painstakingly put together

the prehistoric skeleton over the next seven years.

They use plaster to replicate any bones that are missing or broken.

They carefully drill holes in all of the bones

and attach them together using iron and wire.

Now back together after 145 million years is

the DIPLODOCUS, which was . . .

BOX 21

made complete by the CURATOR,

uncrated by the PREPARATORS,

brought to Washington, D.C. by the MOVERS,

chiseled from the stone by the EXCAVATORS,

authenticated by the PALEONTOLOGIST

and searched for by the DINOSAUR HUNTER.

Here is the

NIGHT WATCHMAN,

making his rounds

in the dark and spooky

back rooms of the museum.

OOPS!

He trips over the

protruding tail of the

just-completed

DIPLODOCUS, which was . . .

put back together by the PREPARATORS and the PALEONTOLOGISTS,

made whole by the CURATOR,

dusted off by the PREPARATORS,

hauled to the train by the MOVERS,

numbered by the EXCAVATORS,

validated by the PALEONTOLOGIST

and hunted down by the DINOSAUR HUNTER.

SECURITY

Here are the **WELDERS**, who custom-build an iron frame
to support the fragile skeleton. They use a special welding machine to fuse the pieces
of the frame together to create a stable structure.

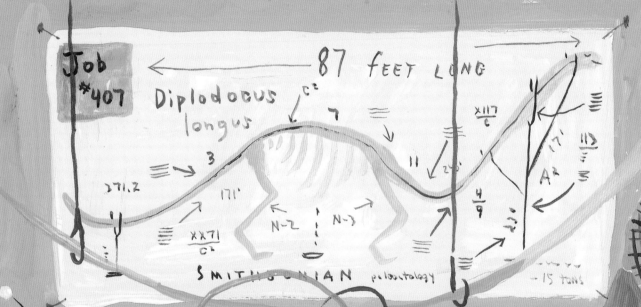

Job #407

Diplodocus longus

87 FEET LONG

SMITHSONIAN paleontology

~ 15 tons

ARC
2-216

Soon to be safely supported—

is the 15-ton

 **DIPLODOCUS**,

which was . . .

tripped over by the NIGHT WATCHMAN,

restored by the PREPARATORS and the PALEONTOLOGISTS,

made complete by the CURATOR,

shellacked by the PREPARATORS,

delivered to Washington, D.C. by the MOVERS,

unearthed by the EXCAVATORS,

certified by the PALEONTOLOGIST

and scouted out by the DINOSAUR HUNTER.

OVALTINE

Here are the museum's **RIGGERS**, who use cranes, hoists, and bobcats to move, position, and pose the 15-ton, 87-foot-long skeleton of the **DIPLODOCUS**, which was . . .

hung from the steel structure by the WELDERS,

stumbled over by the NIGHT WATCHMAN,

put together by the PREPARATORS and PALEONTOLOGISTS,

made complete by the CURATOR,

assembled by the PREPARATORS,

transported by the MOVERS,

excavated by the EXCAVATORS,

checked closely by the PALEONTOLOGIST

and found in crumbling sandstone by the

DINOSAUR HUNTER.

Allosaurus

Here is the museum's **EXHIBITS TEAM**, who paint the background murals, produce the signs, and design the lighting for the **DIPLODOCUS**, which was . . .

Hall of Extinct MONSTERS

DIPLODOCUS
longus

UTAH USA

Late Jurassic

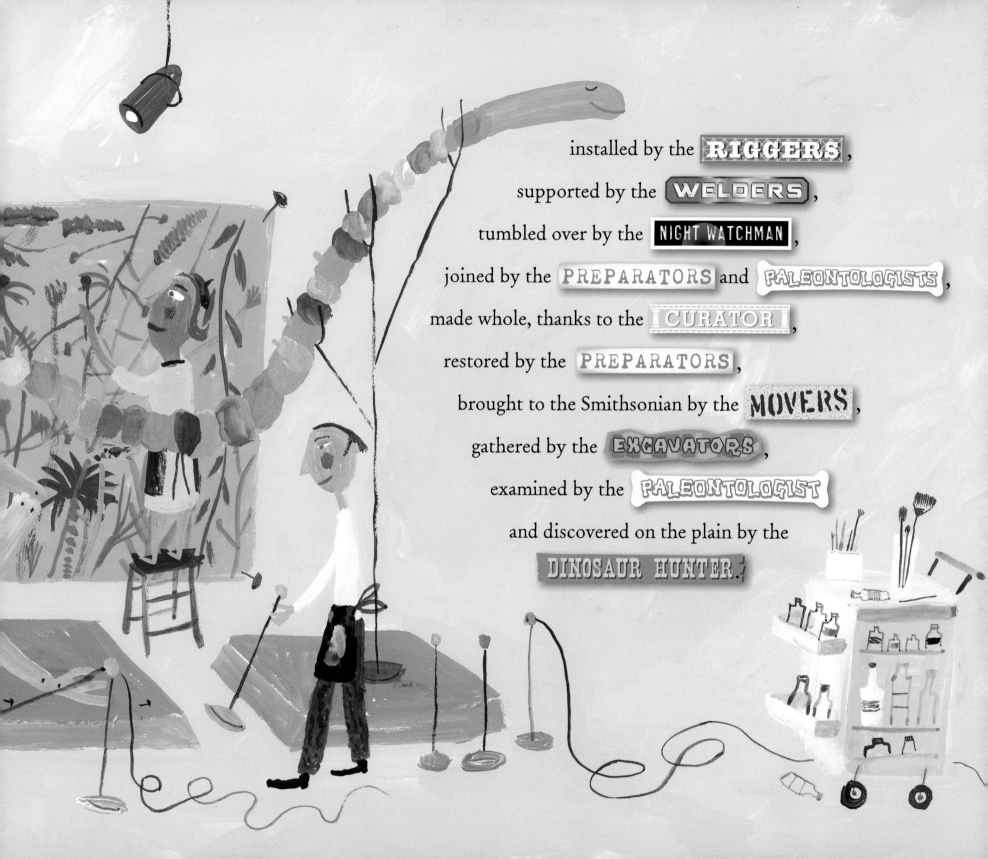

installed by the **RIGGERS**,

supported by the **WELDERS**,

tumbled over by the **NIGHT WATCHMAN**,

joined by the **PREPARATORS** and **PALEONTOLOGISTS**,

made whole, thanks to the **CURATOR**,

restored by the **PREPARATORS**,

brought to the Smithsonian by the **MOVERS**,

gathered by the **EXCAVATORS**,

examined by the **PALEONTOLOGIST**

and discovered on the plain by the

DINOSAUR HUNTER.

Here are the

CLEANERS,

who use soft brushes,

mild soap,

silky chamois,

velvety rags,

and feather dusters

to make spanking-clean for

the opening ceremony the

 **DIPLODOCUS**,

which was . . .

Hall of Extinct MONSTERS

DIPLODOCUS longus

UTAH USA .... Late Jurassic

displayed by the EXHIBITS TEAM,

hoisted by the RIGGERS,

secured safely by the WELDERS,

slipped on by the NIGHT WATCHMAN,

reconstructed by the PREPARATORS and PALEONTOLOGISTS,

made whole by CURATOR,

cleaned up by the PREPARATORS,

shipped to the museum by the MOVERS,

chipped from the stone by the EXCAVATORS,

obtained by the PALEONTOLOGIST

and hunted down by the DINOSAUR HUNTER.

TEE HEE

Paleo TOOTHpaste
* cycadeoid flavor !!

Here is the Smithsonian's **DIRECTOR**,

who makes a speech and gives a toast

at the ribbon-cutting ceremony

for the Museum's newest acquisition:

the **DIPLODOCUS**, which was . . .

washed by the **CLEANERS**,

expertly presented by the **EXHIBITS TEAM**,

moved to the museum floor by the **RIGGERS**,

stabilized by the **WELDERS**,

disturbed by the **NIGHT WATCHMAN**,

pieced together by the **PREPARATORS** and **PALEONTOLOGISTS**,

made whole by the **CURATOR**,

restored by the **PREPARATORS**,

sent from Utah by the **MOVERS**,

amassed by the **EXCAVATORS**,

authenticated by the **PALEONTOLOGIST**

and turned up by the eagle-eyed **DINOSAUR HUNTER**.

A Little Bit of Dino Info

Dinosaurs—from the chicken-sized Compsognathus to the massive 50-ton Brachiosaurus—were reptiles that inhabited the earth for hundreds of millions of years. They lived during the Mesozoic Era, which comprised three geologic time periods: Triassic, 225 to 200 million years ago; Jurassic, 200 to 145 million years ago; and Cretaceous, 145 to 65 million years ago.

Why dinosaurs became extinct 65 million years ago is still a mystery: Did a giant asteroid hit the earth? Did the earth's temperature drop, affecting plant life and making it difficult for dinosaurs to find food? Did volcanic eruptions cause mass extinctions?

The Diplodocus longus (pronounced like this: di-PLOD-o-cus) in this book lived during the late Jurassic period, when the climate was warm, moist, and tropical. Flowering plants flourished, and sea levels were high.

Like all sauropods (a large dinosaur with a small head, long neck and tail, and five-toed limbs—the largest known land animal), the Diplodocus was an herbivore. An herbivore eats only plants. A carnivore eats meat. An omnivore eats all sorts of things. Whatever the diet, dinosaurs were at the top of the food chain.

What's a fossil?

Fossils are the preserved remains, or traces, of an animal, plant, or other living thing from past geologic ages. It can be a skeleton, a footprint, or even a leaf print. The most direct way scientists learn about dinosaurs is by studying fossils, most of which are dug up or excavated from sedimentary rock layers. Usually they can find out when the dinosaur lived by the age of the rock the fossil was found in.

FOSSIL of DINOSAUR tracks

Diplodocus stats

- Diplodocus means "double-beamed" and was named for the double-beamed bones on the underside of its tail

- Average length from tip of head to end of tail: 90 feet long, but could grow as long as 175 feet

- Front legs shorter than back legs

- Eyes located on either side of its head

- Teeth shaped like pencils

- Tail had more than 80 bones

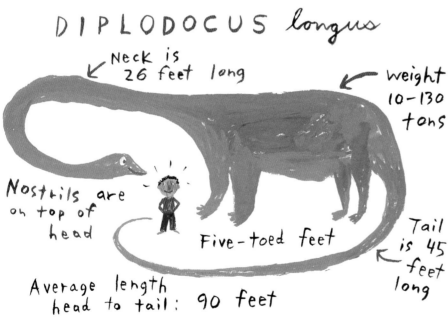

DIPLODOCUS longus

Neck is 26 feet long

weight 10-130 tons

Nostrils are on top of head

Five-toed feet

Tail is 45 feet long

Average length head to tail: 90 feet

At The Museum

This book is about the particular story, or journey, behind an artifact. In museum-speak, the word for this is the *provenance*.

It is thought that the Diplodocus was about 45 years old when it died. It is not known whether it was male or female.

This Diplodocus is 87 feet long as restored, but should actually be 100 feet long. The original preparators did not take into account the missing cartilage between the vertebrae.

The replaced parts were painted to blend in with the real bones, but not exactly, as it's important to be able to tell the difference between what's real and what's fake. If you visit the Smithsonian National Museum of Natural History in Washington, D.C., try and see yourself which bones are the 'real things.' Or you can go to the Smithsonian's dinosaur website: **www.paleobiology.si.edu/dinosaurs**.

Some museums have only castings of skeletons. As you've just read, this Diplodocus is (mostly) made up of actual fossils (real bones) and therefore is an original specimen for a species. The word for this is *holotype*.

Behind the Discovery

Earl
DOUGLASS

The dinosaur hunter that appears in the book is paleontologist **EARL DOUGLASS** (1862-1931), who worked at the Carnegie Museum in Pittsburgh, Pennsylvania. In 1909, he discovered the Carnegie Quarry, which is now known as the Dinosaur National Monument, in Utah. This discovery was said to be one of the most extensive in the history of paleontology for the number of fossils that were excavated.

Charles W.
GILMORE

The paleontologist that is featured in the book is **CHARLES W. GILMORE** (1874-1945), who worked for the U.S. National Museum (Smithsonian) from 1903 until his death. He was first hired as a preparator to work on the Owen C. Marsh (another well-known paleontologist) dinosaur collection, and then later became curator of fossil reptiles.

The very first dinosaur bones, found in the 1600's, were thought to be from a giant man! A bit later, dinosaur bones were assumed to be from giant ravens freed from Noah's Ark. "Dinosaur" means "terrible lizard," but dinosaurs were not lizards at all. In fact, the animal of today that most closely resembles the dinosaur is the bird.

Here I am visiting a Diplodocus excavation in Wyoming. The paleontologists told me that a real dinosaur bone fragment will stick to your tongue because it's porous.

The quarry in Utah where this Diplodocus was found is now part of Dinosaur National Monument, and you can visit the park: **www.nps.gov/dino/index.htm**.

Check out these Dino Dig websites:

You and your family can be part of a real dinosaur dig!

www.DinosaurAcademy.com
www.MTDINOTRAIL.ORG

RIBBON

to the HALL of EXTINCT MONSTERS

glue

FRENCH Champagne